Playing in the Park

Jillian Powell

W

FRANKLIN WATTS

LONDON · SYDNEY

First published in 2005 by
Franklin Watts
96 Leonard Street
London
EC2A 4XD

Franklin Watts Australia
45-51 Huntley Street
Alexandria, NSW 2015

Editor: Rachel Tonkin
Series design: Mo Choy
Art director: Jonathan Hair
Photography: Chris Fairclough
PSHE Consultant: Wendy Anthony

A CIP catalogue record for this book is
available from the British Library

ISBN: 0 7496 6048 1

Printed in Hong Kong

Contents

In the park 4

Your turn, my turn 6

Waiting for your go 8

Sharing 10

Being polite 12

Saying sorry 14

Helping others 16

Keep it tidy 18

Staying safe 20

Think about . . . 22

Index 24

In the park

Going to the park is fun.
There are lots of things
to see and do.

You share the park with other people. It's important to think of them when you are playing.

? What do you like doing when you go to the park?

5

Your turn, my turn

You should take turns with your family and friends so that everyone has a go.

This way, everyone will have fun and no-one will feel left out.

Take turns

Waiting for your go

Sometimes you need to be patient and wait in line for your go.

?

What would happen
if everyone tried to go down
the slide at the same time?

This way, everyone gets a turn
and it's safer, too. Always wait
for your go at a safe distance.

Sharing

Everyone enjoys sharing a ball.
It helps you make friends.

You can have fun sharing
a play area, too.

Making friends

Being polite

When you ask to join in a game, always remember to ask politely. It helps to say please and thank you, too.

Please

What do you say when a friend offers to share something with you?

Saying sorry

You should try not to upset
anyone with things you
say or do.

If you do upset someone, think about their feelings. Say sorry to show that you care.

How does it make you feel when a friend is mean to you but doesn't say sorry?

Helping others

There are lots of things you can do to help other people in the park.

If you are kind and helpful, it will make the park a nicer place for everyone.

? How could you help someone who has lost their football?

Keep it tidy

You should always remember to clear up your litter in the park. Litter can be dangerous for the birds and animals that live there.

Keep the park tidy by
using the litter bins.

Staying safe

There are lots of people in the park and you need to be careful. Don't talk to strangers or take anything from them.

Be careful

? What should you do if a stranger offers you sweets or a ride home?

You should always stay near the people you are with. Do not wander off on your own.

Think about . . .

When you're playing on the swings, there are lots of things you should think about . . .

? How do you ask politely if you can have a go on the swings?

? How do you feel if other children don't let you play on the swings, too?

? How should you ask your parent or friend to give you a push on the swings?

? Why should you be careful on the swings and not push people off or get in their way?

Think about why manners matter when you want to buy an ice cream . . .

? How do you ask your parent if you can have an ice cream?

? What should you do if there is a big queue for ice creams?

? What do you say to the ice cream seller when you buy an ice cream?

? If a stranger asks if you want an ice cream, what do you say?

Index

family 6

feelings 15

friends 5, 6, 10, 13

game 12

helping 16, 17

kind 17

patient 8

please 12

polite 12, 13, 22

queue 23

safe 9, 20, 21

sharing 5, 10, 11, 13

sorry 14, 15

strangers 20, 23

swings 22

thank you 12

tidy 18, 19

turns 6, 7, 9

waiting 8

Author Biographies

Beatrix Potter

Charlotte Guillain

www.raintreepublishers.co.uk
Visit our website to find out
more information about
Raintree books.

To order:

☎ Phone 0845 6044371

📄 Fax +44 (0) 1865 312263

💻 Email myorders@raintreepublishers.co.uk

Customers from outside the UK please telephone +44 1865 312262

Raintree is an imprint of Capstone Global Library Limited,
a company incorporated in England and Wales having its
registered office at 7 Pilgrim Street, London, EC4V 6LB
– Registered company number: 6695582

Text © Capstone Global Library Limited 2012
First published in hardback in 2012
The moral rights of the proprietor have been asserted.

Edited by Rebecca Rissman, Daniel Nunn,
  and Sian Smith
Designed by Joanna Hinton-Malivoire
Picture research by Tracy Cummins
Production by Victoria Fitzgerald
Originated by Capstone Global Library Ltd
Printed and bound in China by South China
  Printing Company Ltd

ISBN 978 1 406 23451 0
15 14 13 12 11
10 9 8 7 6 5 4 3 2 1

British Library Cataloguing in Publication Data
Guillain, Charlotte.
Beatrix Potter. – (Author biographies)
1. Potter, Beatrix, 1866-1943–Pictorial works–   Juvenile
literature. 2. Authors, English–20th century–
Biography–Pictorial works–Juvenile literature. 3. Women
authors, English–20th century–Biography–Pictorial works–
Juvenile literature.
  I. Title II. Series
  823.9'12-dc22

Acknowledgements
We would like to thank the following for permission
to reproduce photographs: Alamy Images pp. 5 (©
UrbanZone), 9, 18 (© The National Trust Photolibrary), 14
(© David Cheshire), 15 (© Pictorial Press Ltd), 20 (© David
Taylor); The Beatrix Potter Society pp. 6, 7 (Rupert Potter);
Getty Images pp. 4 (Express Newspapers), 8 (Rupert
Potter/Time Life Pictures), 10 (Hulton Archive), 17 left
(Andy Craword); Glow Images pp. 16, 23c (Westend61/
Nabiha Dahhan); The Kobal Collection p. 21 (Weinstein
Co); Newscom p. 19 (handout/KRT); Rex USA p. 11 (NILS
JORGENSEN); Shutterstock pp. 12 (© wim claes), 13 (©
mamahoohooba), 17 right, 23h (© Julie Boro), 23a (©
Karel Gallas), 23b (© Petro Feketa), 23e (© Kevin Eaves),
23f (© Vasily Smirnov), 23g (© Falconia).

Cover photograph of Beatrix Potter pictured outside her
Lake District house near Ambleside reproduced with
permission of Getty Images (Popperfoto). Back cover
image of a rabbit in meadow reproduced with permission
of Shutterstock (wim claes).

Every effort has been made to contact copyright holders
of material reproduced in this book. Any omissions will be
rectified in subsequent printings if notice is given to the
publisher.

Contents

Who was Beatrix Potter?. 4

Where did she grow up? 6

What did she do before she was
     a writer? 8

How did she start writing books?. 10

What books did she write? 12

What did she write about? 14

How did Beatrix draw the pictures in
     her books? 16

What else did she like to do? 18

Why is she famous today?. 20

Timeline of Beatrix Potter's life and work . 22

Glossary 23

Find out more 24

Index 24

Some words are shown in bold, **like this**. You can find them in the glossary on page 23.

Who was Beatrix Potter?

Beatrix Potter was a writer and **illustrator**.

She wrote and drew the pictures for children's books.

Beatrix Potter wrote many books that we still read today.

Her most famous book is *The Tale of Peter Rabbit*.

Where did she grow up?

Beatrix Potter was born in 1866.

She grew up in London, England.

Beatrix had one brother, who went away to boarding school.

Like many girls at that time, she did not go to school.

What did she do before she was a writer?

Beatrix loved painting when she was a child.

She had lots of pets and liked to draw and paint them.

She also liked to write in a **diary**.

She used a secret code so that nobody else could understand it.

How did she start writing books?

In 1893 Beatrix wrote a story in a letter to a sick boy.

She drew pictures for the story and called it *The Tale of Peter Rabbit*.

Beatrix decided to make the story into a book and **printed** 250 copies.

Then a company **published** the book and she became famous.

What books did she write?

Beatrix wrote many other famous books.

She wrote several stories about rabbits, such as *The Tale of Benjamin Bunny*.

She also wrote *The Tale of Squirrel Nutkin* and *The Tale of Jemima Puddle-Duck*.

Children love to read about her funny animal **characters**.

What did she write about?

Beatrix bought a farm in the Lake District, in Cumbria.

Many of her stories are set in the countryside around her farm.

Many people thought she didn't have a normal life for a woman at that time.

She often wrote about animals that didn't follow the rules, like her.

How did Beatrix draw the pictures in her books?

Some of Beatrix's pictures are black and white.

She drew these pictures using pen and ink, like the artist in the photo.

Other pictures in her books are in colour.

She painted these pictures using paints called **watercolours**.

What else did she like to do?

Beatrix ran several farms in the Lake District.

She raised animals, such as sheep, on her farms.

She looked after nature and animals all her life.

She also loved painting **landscapes** in the countryside.

Why is she famous today?

People still buy Beatrix Potter's books today.

There are many Beatrix Potter gifts and toys.

There are museums and galleries on her life and work.

People have made films about her life and her books, too.

Timeline of Beatrix Potter's life and work

1866   Beatrix Potter was born in London.

1893   She wrote *The Tale of Peter Rabbit.*

1901   She **published** *The Tale of Peter Rabbit.*

1905   She bought Hill Top Farm.

1913   She got married.

1930   Her last book, *The Tale of Little Pig Robinson,* was published.

1943   Beatrix Potter died.

Glossary

 **character** person or animal in a story

 **diary** a book where someone writes down what they have done each day

 **illustrator** person who draws or paints pictures to go with a story

 **landscape** scenery

 **print** make many copies of something, for example a book

 **published** made into a book or put in a magazine and printed

 **watercolour** a type of paint

Find out more

Books

Some of Beatrix Potter's books: *The Tale of Peter Rabbit*, *The Tale of Squirrel Nutkin*, *The Tale of Jemima Puddle-Duck*, *The Tale of Benjamin Bunny*, *The Tale of Pigling Bland*, *The Tale of Mrs Tiggy-Winkle*, *The Tale of Two Bad Mice*, and *The Tale of Tom Kitten*.

Websites

http://www.hop-skip-jump.com/

Visit this website to find out more about Beatrix Potter and the World of Beatrix Potter attraction in the Lake District, Cumbria.

Index

animal 8, 12, 13, 15, 18, 19, 23

book 4, 5, 10–13, 17, 20, 21, 22

characters 13, 23

countryside 14, 19

farm 14, 18, 22

Lake District 14, 18

picture 4, 16–17, 23

watercolour 17, 23